NAUSIKAA'S ISLE

NAUSIKAA'S ISLE

Design by Rebecca Chamlee
Front cover photo by Gianluca Muratori.
Back cover photo Giorgio Tavernari, collage by Courtney Gregg

www.postmediabooks.it

ISBN 9788874901425
PRINTED IN ITALY

Nausikaa's ISLE

A Tribute to Paul Vangelisti

Edited & *with an* Introduction *by* Dennis Phillips

POSTMEDIA ●BOOKS

MILAN

2015

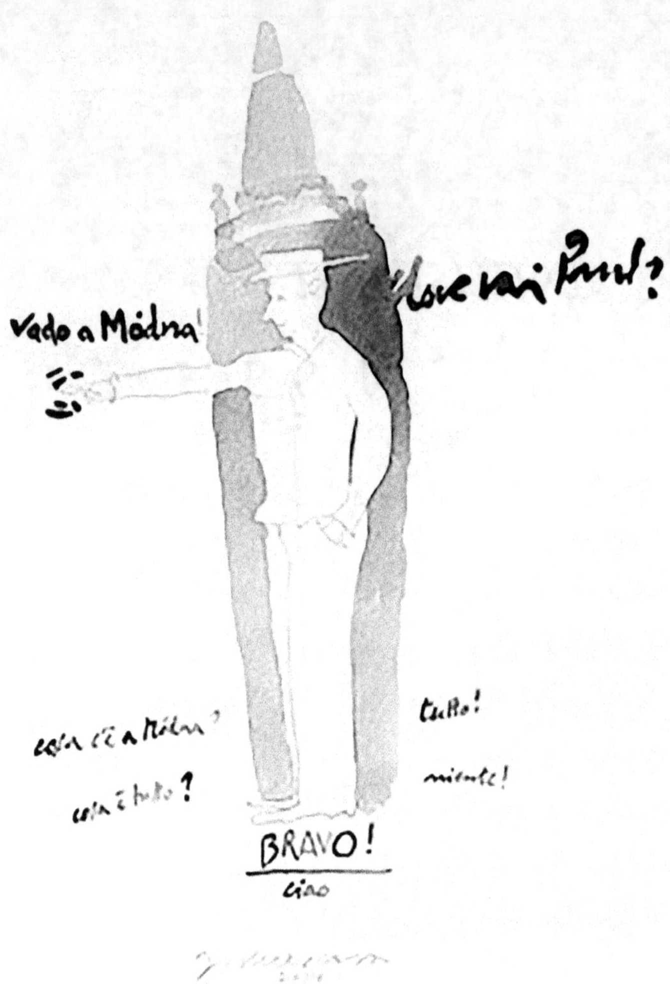

Giuliano Della Casa

Giuliano Della Casa once caught Paul Vangelisti napping and made a sketch. It's a peaceful enough likeness—one that Douglas Messerli added to the cover of one of his anthologies—but I suspect Della Casa was inspired by wanting to preserve such a rare sight. That the sketch echoes Wyndham Lewis' portrait of a sleeping Ezra Pound adds extra resonance, because, like Pound, Vangelisti is apparently tireless.

The reservoir of energy that fuels his drive is well-known to his many collaborators, to his students, to his friends and to the contributors to this volume. Those who know him purely through his multifarious work may understand how mass can equal energy. When I've been asked to introduce him at, say, a reading or lecture, I have fallen upon a fact that attests to this energy: most mortals would be happy to have mastered any one of Vangelisti's portfolio of masteries.[*] As a poet, a translator, an editor, a publisher, an educator, and, for all the right reasons, an administrator, Paul Vangelisti has created a force of gravity felt by his readers, several international generations of poets, and his students, that brings to mind the similar influence of Pound.

One way Vangelisti's energy manifests itself in his gift for elevating the ordinary. He somehow creates an aura of importance around even the simplest of daily interactions, whether its meeting for a quick coffee or spending the evening plotting a collaboration. I don't mean a heavy, self-conscious, over-determined kind of importance; nor do I mean a personal, puffed-up, self-importance.[**] What I mean is he never gives in to the overwhelming pressures that would extinguish literature in general and

---

[*] "Mastery" lately seems beached on the shore of disapproval. The life work of Vangelisti testifies to the ephemeral nature of this new judgment.

[**] Quite the contrary. In fact, as one measure, consider this personal observation: In my three plus decades working in the environment of an Art College, Vangelisti is the only person who, once elevated to the high position of "Department Chair," remained completely unchanged (except for several extra measures of exasperation), where all others, in one way or another, seemed to inflate with their perceived potency, usually atmospheres beyond themselves.

poetry in particular. He sustains those in his orbits with his matter-of-fact belief that what they are doing is significant; that history, some version of history, is in the making as they work together, eat and drink together, speak together; that history is made in the doing of what is deeply believed by those with the sincerity to do those things well.[*]

The notion of elevating the ordinary is also a lens through which both the *fact* of his accomplishments and the *fabric* of his own writing may be seen. There, in the books that comprise the impressive list of his poetic works, is a world that never strays far from facts on the ground. Place anchors his work, ballasts it, zeros it in. But if place is a mooring line for Vangelisti, it's sometimes a cable with a clear connection to its vessel, and sometimes a thread, tethering a more distant object, at times afloat, at times soaring high above the horizon.[**]

The one thing Paul Vangelisti is decidedly not expert at is retiring. And though this volume is meant to commemorate two milestones that he's reaching simultaneously—his 70th birthday and his stepping down as Founding Chair of the Graduate Writing Program at Otis College of Art and Design—"retirement" is here used only as a convention that marks a transition, one that, if an editor may be allowed an editorial comment, will benefit the worlds of poetry and translation and publishing, since he will now be able to shuffle off the time-killing coils of administration and internecine small college politics for his more sublime occupations.

So, in tribute, recognition and thanks for his momentous contributions to poetry, publishing, translating, teaching, and for his unflagging energy in bringing people together and ideas into reality, this volume. The reader will soon see that this is not a festschrift, at least not in the traditional sense of the word

---

[*] In that, one can see how deeply integrated in his work—and I mean *all* his work—are the poetic and the political.

[**] Another way of making the connection to his relationship to the quotidian is through his long series of "alphabet poems." In reference to his *Two* (Talisman, 2013) I wrote that "…Vangelisti's ongoing exploration of the alphabet, [is] an arena as terrifying in its vastness as it is familiar in its coordinates. The alphabet's armature of constraint combined with Vangelisti's unmatched formal acumen creates the ground on which the poet shifts through an encyclopedic array of concerns using the lens of poetic reason. What emerges is a poetry of economy and strength, compelling in its unique voicing and constantly generative of ideas and observations."

(with a couple of exceptions at the end of the book.) It is, instead, an anthology of some of the writers and artists with whom Vangelisti has worked the closest. The simple idea was to compile some work that Paul would like, that Paul has supported, as a way of saluting him at this moment of transition. It opens with "Extracts," by four deceased colleagues of great importance to him, and ends with a couple of recollections. Between are poetry, fiction and visual art that suggest Vangelisti's wide-ranging concerns and his ceaseless advocacy.

At the very beginning of the volume stands Nausikaa at the estuary of her island, beckoning, full of desire, always just out of reach, always the catalyst for the story that follows.

Dennis Phillips
Spring 2015

Courtney Gregg

E X T R A C T S

Moskovskaya (vodka)

for Paul Vangelisti

The fan its enchanted movement
from films with gracious legendary actors
islands typhoons volcanoes seaplanes
the balcony in bloom slowly stirs
with the railing printed on the hills
it's the cocktail decorated with leaves
of mint of lime of maple or mulberry
with rose petals if the vodka is rosy
effect obtained with the juice of a peach
sprayed to mark the expanse of snow
next to big rivers blossoming with caviar
better to eat it with boiled potatoes
a little butter and some fresh onion
the parsley is starting to invade the terrace
jungle suited to Japanese triumphs
of the overwrought flyer who's going mad
of the happy prisoner screaming he feels bad
ejaculating he dreamed of his wife
leaning on an out-of-tune piano
in the stench of tropical sweat
buzzing of insects and animal cries
the fan provides little relief
with its sensible turning hour after hour
in the cocktail the ice is starting to melt
the vodka is pale as denatured blood.

(trans. P.V.)

Of course

Whilst I still can.
Whilst. I do.
Whilst the otter to the edge of the pond
Whilst

(I have never seen an otter)

Whilst the midnight of morning
Holds me close
Whilst all dogs are quiet
(especially the birds)
Whilst the hush of a new day
allows no helicopters
and prayer is silent.

Whilst memories yet hold me prisoner
of my hulk, whilst Whitman yet holds
such daring of his & lord of his affection.
When silence pervades

and any punctuation is unnecessary.

(as a child I was told "you think too much."
Parentheses rarely apply.

Whilst monsters (be there any)
are asleep whilst the mind slumbers, it seems.

And the day is good.
And doubt is a Haloween pumpkin

without a candle
(in it.

Looking for Seven Mistakes in the Same Film Seen Twice in a Row

1. In the first screening|
   the level of passion
   was higher.
2. The genital research
   went much deeper.
3. The second kiss was longer.
4. The unbearableness
   of the narcissistic wound
   was minor.
5. The second screening,
   in the sequence with their first
   meeting,
   there was less enthusiasm.
6. (His member seemed to me shorter.)
7. Then they changed
   the furniture
   switched
   the paintings
   she
   couldn't any longer
   surrender herself completely
   then
   she's missing a shoe
   has one less finger
   has one less arm
   with her missing legs
   she goes off into the void
   and
   there's nothing more to see

(trans. P.V)

All Songs are Crazy

Some are beautiful.
Who could sing
All the songs we know?
How many of us that can, know
How many of those who sing know
What singing is.
So I who have sung and heard song
Want to know the singers
And the song
I who have learned singing from the oldest singers
In the world and have sung some songs myself
Want to create that song that everybody knows
And that everybody will sing one day.
So what is left to do? That is how the song
Begins.

NAUSIKAA'S ISLE

NAUSIKAA'S ISLE

Roy Dowell

Duck Lake

That beautiful lamp
the way it comes into focus, a
narrowing, tightening

this moment of recognition

and I saw
a few times
what some thought
they saw

the dream world is for dreamers

"Let's spit on Hegel"—Carla Lonzi

What is the nature of the relationship between the elves and wild boars?
Where does Noah stand in the Ark? Who are the dancing Maenads? When
will a silver birch tree grow in the kitchen[*]?

---

[*] This birch tree is already growing. Cf. *Wormwood Forest*, Mary Mycio.

Seven fugues on the art of escape

fuga n. 15

ma poi vien sempre l'occhio di un'apertura
lo slargo intravisto dove la fuga s'impenna
in transito scarlatto
e il piatto ride

fuga n. 21

concedi dunque
poiché ci hai sopraffatto
fuga codarda e furore intatto

fuga n. 28

non c'è errore né eccesso tra le spire
evasive dello slancio come sai imperfetto
nient'altro in fondo che il fondo e noi lesti
di scatto in fuorigioco sì, sappiamo
che c'inviti grazioso alla cautela
ma si fa presto a dire prudenza se la fuga riviene alla partenza

fuga n. 31

transito passo fuga che non torna
epperò solo la soglia di un caffè grigiodolce educato
benvenuto a nessuno niente sorpresa e niente ardori
mordere per fuggire, cari,
o son dolori

fuga n. 37

in fuga immobile dove si fiacca la somma inesistenza come
per caso incauto magari un'improvvida presenza e senza
riflesso rimargine figurarsi un appello
– ci dicono che sei dappertutto dev'essere per questo
che non ti si trova mai

fuga n. 45

darsi alla fuga vuol dire naturalmente
che del tuo assenso non c'importa niente

non confondere il passo di fuga a una quieta
deriva d'occasione
– di scarto l'ombra dell'ora rilancia in ombra
pesta e che il terzo non sia dato non c'importa
granché se poi non arriva un quarto a scompigliare le file

Paris — Magomadas, August 2014

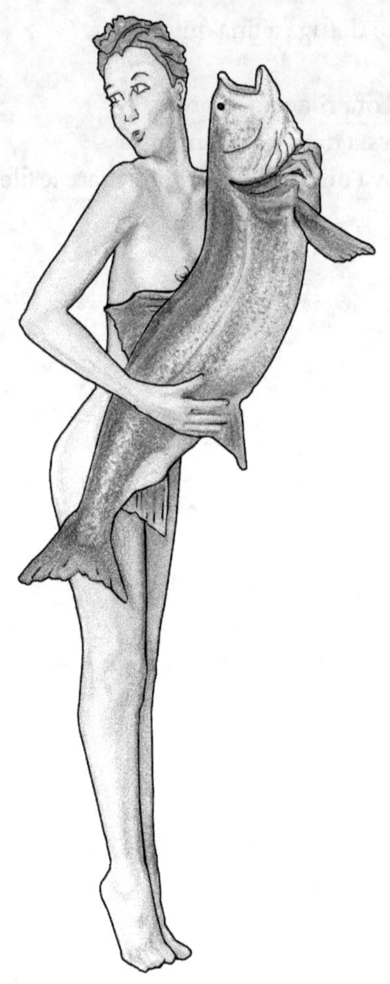

Shelly Forbes

An Old Italian Saying (for Paul Vangelisti)

My uncle was always wary of vegetarians, and the summer before I left for college, he told me not to become one. There was an old Italian saying, he said, that it would do me well to make my motto: *Eat* it *before* it *eats you.* And then he said something like, You're a good kid—we never have to worry about you. This wasn't entirely true: I was not always so good.

In the late afternoons that August, I'd bike up to Vermont Canyon and try to pick up a match, which was a little foolish given the record heat, so dry you could hear the bark twisting off of the eucalyptus that ringed the tennis courts. I was often the only person out there. But one day after I had practiced my serve and was resting in the shade, an odd-looking fellow appeared and asked if I wanted to hit a few balls while I waited for whomever I was expecting. I explained I was on my own and said sure why not. My guess was this guy was in his late thirties, and he looked like, in my uncle's parlance, a real crumbum: Baggy shorts, rumpled shirt, a goofy white headband with matching wristbands. His game was sloppy, too. He framed two balls in a row and netted two after that. He apologized, said he was rusty, and managed to hit a few weak forehands. He waved me into the net and told me that the only way he could ever play half-decently was if he were playing for points. Would I play a set? He won the toss, served two-double faults, won a point on a pathetic short backhand, and I easily put away his next two serves. I wasn't even hitting great shots, but this guy couldn't move his feet. He was sluggish and already sunburned.

On the changeover I learned he sold insurance. He was in the business of leading folks away from risk, but he himself wasn't averse to a little wagering now and then. What did I think about making a bet on the set, say twenty bucks? I had that much in my pocket. We shook on it. I served well enough to win a love game, but these were only second serves I was making. He lost the next game, again only picking up one point, a net-ball at that. So I was up three-love when he said we needed to make this more interesting. He wanted to up the bet to a hundred dollars. I told him I didn't feel comfortable taking his money, and also I didn't have that much on me. He said we could go to my bank if I lost, and anyway I probably wasn't going to lose. He'd put the first twenty under his racket cover on the bench and made a big show of withdrawing four more twenties and adding them to the pot, all of this before I shook his hand again, which I did. His hand was rough and calloused.

I began serving again and a funny thing happened: The guy's groundstrokes became clean and flat and hard. Our rallies went longer and he hit two backhand-down-the-line winners. Suddenly the guy had an inside-out shot, controlling points from the ad corner, and after he broke me, guess what? He had a crazy kick serve-into-the-body that I could barely get my racket on. He was up three-two, broke me and held—now *he* was up four-three. He said he was getting some lucky balls was all, but it should be no surprise that he then broke me and was up five-three and poised to win the hundred dollars.

Before I served, I told him I needed some incentive. Did he have another hundred in his pocket? Because we should double the bet. That's a lot of money for you, kid, he said, and I said indeed it was. So: Two hundred for the set? And he squinted at me a moment and rubbed his nose, and when he smiled, I could see his teeth had been yellowed by cheap diner coffee, years and years of it. A life on the road was a hard life, I thought.

His first serve, I read his toss: I got around the ball and hit a forehand winner crosscourt. The guy chuckled. He went down the center on his next serve, and I put away this ball, too. Now the guy looked at me with some concern. I broke him at love. I said I was getting some lucky balls was all, but that didn't explain the serves I started to fire off. After my second ace, he called me a son-of-a-bitch. After my top-spun forehand winner high to his backhand, and then another ace, he called me a motherfucker. We were at five-all. I broke him easily, went up six-five, and at the changeover he said he would never renege on a bet, that wasn't his style, but he wanted to know what was going on. Was I playing him for some kind of fool? Was I playing *him*?

My uncle had warned me about shady characters who once upon a time used to wander up to the courts on late summer afternoons looking for marks. I didn't believe that such people existed, but then again, maybe they did. I'd been waiting for this very moment for weeks. I'd played varsity tennis three years in high school and was heading up north on an athletic scholarship. You had to be a very good player to look like a lousy player, and this guy, this crumbum, he was very good. But I was better. What I said to him after I won the next game and pocketed the two hundred dollars was that my uncle had taught me an old Italian saying, and I think the guy thought I was a little lunatic, but he did grin briefly. He also said his family was Italian, too, and *Eat* it *before* it *eats you* was not an expression he'd ever heard from any relatives. Over the years, I've asked around wherever I've traveled, and I will admit that on this point, I believe the hustler whom I hustled was probably right. No matter, these are still words to live by.

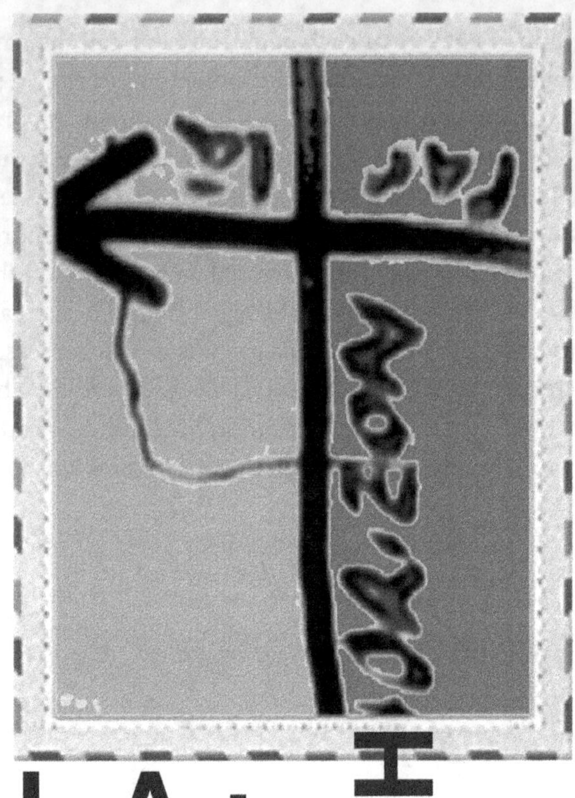

L.A.: II

Souvenirs d'une pêche à l'aube, loin ➔ ➔
(Tiziano, Maurizio & Adriano) Paul et moi .

➜ ➜ de L.A. en partant de port San Pedro avec les frères Spatola
The horizon is on the other side !

Julien Blaine (juin 2014)

Julie Blaine

Nausikaa's Isle
A Tribute to Paul Vangelisti

Whose Transbluesency?

The bamboo thirst.

Before jet, then cone, then shower, then purgatory.

The Allen Rufus, its magenta and orange collar in full view, hovers,
whistle-darts. Because, in this city of farce, one fidgets to see clearly.
You are the presence of Colombia, post Chibcha Indios, praeter Colón,
deflecting Bólivar.

Down Valentine. One Fix, two fix, head fix, news fix, and every $6 cup of joe
is a reminder that it pays to be a hip kind of blue. Only no one here
remembers Coltrane being beaten up by Miles after he was told not to play
like a white guy.

Left. And the echo here from Echo Park Boulevard all too familiar with its
presence of mind to lead with an offer.

Sunday. Left on Alessandro, right on Glendale. The Two, to the Five, to the
105, and south toward the sun that will take us into tomorrow, sporting
pneumatic heart valves. Each syncopating doubletime, but the odds don't
add up—I'm driving west and I can't get even.

Whose transbluesency, whose pillar of this community?
Who?

Bats, on high. The fog nestling over Dodger Stadium. Surrounding lights
from homes upon homes gas-lit.

And the pendulum swings, as palimpsest rolls west to the arroyo seco, a devil
of an earthquake, the chill of civil unrest, and pines for the Pacific.

Old Music

for Paul

sandpaper walls
fell over light rain
through Bagnone's
Medieval passageways
until the sun god
appeared on an old man's
face where

several cars were
stationed as if by
command—in a café
men trimmed lilacs
and sank their eyes
into the darker mysterious
of their lives

nobody said anything
clouds re-appeared
an hour later
a heavy rain as we
turned on the stove
in a tiny kitchen

id

entity

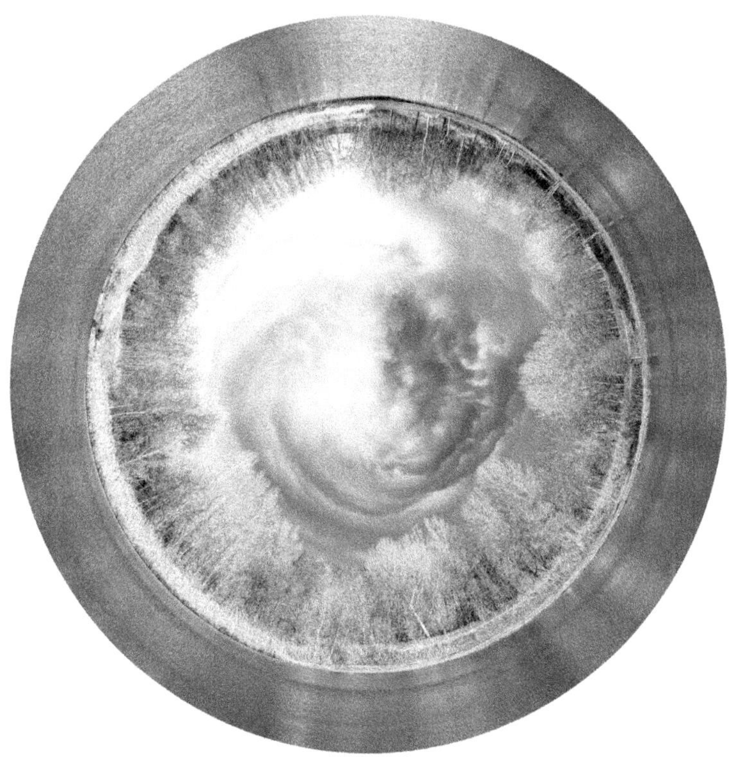

Gianluca Muratori

Nausikaa's Isle
A Tribute to Paul Vangelisti

from *Serial*

Donnelly rolled his metal chair away from the desk, leaned back and stretched. Carl Turner's file lay open in front of him. A defective florescent light hummed overhead. Memos had flown back and forth about the hum for weeks, but somehow, it was still there. Donnelly remembered the walk to the Chambers Street Station. The sun was just beginning to paint the eastern sky and for a moment, even the traffic noise had ceased, leaving the great Avenues blank and still, like blackboards washed clean for the start of school. Donnelly couldn't escape the feeling that Art was going to tell him something, but the walk had been mostly silent, almost brooding. Art asked Donnelly to forward mail to his new address. Donnelly had nodded and, as the subway entrance came into view, Donnelly, to his surprise, had choked up.

He couldn't say exactly when Art began to speak, but he was aware, an hour later, of the two of them standing to the left of a river of people flowing down into the subway. Yet the only sound Donnelly heard was Art's soft, throaty voice. "It's not even that they don't have the language to tell you what's happening to them, because some of them do. It's because language itself has broken down. I know what you're thinking. Am I, the advocate of language, the great reader… is it Art saying this? But what I'm talking about is a deeper breakdown, at the medullar level, between word and act, a breakdown as cosmic as their linkage is in Genesis. Why, what we're dealing with is no less than a primordial disbelief in the power of words to contain reality. That's why your average serial killer resorts to terror, then pain, and finally, because he can't even believe in his victims' screams, to death. Death resolves the problem of unbelief. You have to believe that someone is dead. There are circumstances where you just can't fake it."

Art had paused and blown his great red nose, famous in the department as the organ of truth and proof. Then, carefully folding his handkerchief, he'd patted Donnelly on the shoulder looked past him at a gusher of humanity erupting from the subway, and said, gnomically: "Always look for the story teller." And like that, he was gone, visible for a second like a cork bobbing against an onrushing tide, then utterly and completely gone. Oh, he sent postcards as he said he would, but Art himself was missing from them. They could have been written by the mailman. As it was, they were written to no-one, or to an imaginary colleague whose imaginary interest in Art they addressed and mocked. "Hi boys. Another sunny day. Off to catch the big one. Art." "Hi guys. Cold enough for you? Water 82 Degrees. Keep those cards and letters coming. Art." After a while, Donnelly stopped reading them. And a while after that, they stopped coming.

Three Happy Old-Age-Frisbees

for Paul

Lo strumento (con sopra disegnato
un omino supino, le ginocchia
piegate, tre pulsanti sopra e tre sotto),
per alzare o abbassare il mio letto
d'ospedale in tre diversi punti,
è costruito dalla società Hill-Rom
(Zingari della collina?)
e ha nome…
ha nome
AvantGuard.
(Dentro mi risuona una risata irresistibile).
E' questa la versione contemporanea
degli dei che comunicano coi personaggi
epici? Quelli di Omero, per fare un esempio?

*

In seconda media, fissando
le macchie d'inchiostro
e i buchi dei tarli del mio
vecchio banco di legno,
mi chiedevo: ma come può
Ulisse aver vissuto così
intensamente, così compiutamente
e noi qui, ora, così… così
comuni, ordinari, "predestinati"?

*

Mi sbagliavo. Non è questione
di tempo. Di duemila anni di
differenza, né di quei particolari

e spesso magici eventi esterni.
Audacia, sofferenza, *pazienza*
e poi anni di lavoro in miniera
per prendere coscienza di tutto ciò
che si è fatto (di giusto e di sbagliato)
e del perché…
e *finalmente,* quasi alla fine
vieni accontentato.
Capisci la metafora che Omero
ci ha dato. Il modello epico.
Sempre possibile. Mai cambiato.

Cenotaph for Separation Anxiety

When I was young, the mother tongue, as old
as stones—huge lumps and slabs of it on mountainsides
5,000 feet and up—immoveable as fire-scoured cones
of earth-enveloped roots—seemed utterly incomprehensible;
and now, with more beneficence than I deserve,
I hear the supple youthfulness of syllables
inviting me to strop a promissory map
for those still yearning: "Come on in. You look
like you live here. If not, make yourself at home."

Cenotaph for a Migrant Halfway There

Imagine bare hands in an ice-chest
Striated with freshly-gutted fish:
If memory of hunger could numb,
She could've walked a second continent.
Imagine the slosh of melted time:
Satiety as gorgeous as a rhyme.

Audiovisual Requests

Men and women with rising voices, near-mint
sets of secondhand perspectives, with a commitment,
and a very strong one, to the kind of honest poetry
that rarely exposes its own internal operations.

A just and noble cause, one that knows, almost
by heart, when to revise and when to submit, when
to quote and, more importantly, from where, when to hit
the market, as tough as it may be, with a killer cover letter.

Nothing compares to the pleasure
of captive audiences of two or three
or more than one acceptance.

Almost like getting to know
Jesus Christ
on a first-name basis.

Rising stars with various degrees, near-fine
men and women with the confidence
that you will find them fascinating, searching,
as they often do, for the perfect slideshow.

A noble quest, one that knows almost no rejections,
only the occasional revise and resubmit, provided,
of course, that not too many references are made
to the kind of poetry that questions its own utilitarian value.

Nothing compares to the pleasure
of a comparative epiphany, economically
articulated in twenty minutes or less.

Almost like receiving
an honorary degree
from Mount Sinai.

Anything to Please

Professors of poetry to make a commitment
not to commit a mathematical not
to mention logical atrocity when calculating
participation grades, especially the odd
extra point because, after all, five out of five
makes no sense, no sense at all, even
if other professors do it, and they do it
all the time.

Professors of poetry to post clear
and consistent criteria, rubrics, outcomes,
objectives, lecture notes, especially
lecture notes because who wants to
actually, if you will pardon the split infinitive,
come to class or write things down or contact
two or three reliable friends when you can
circumvent the text with elegance and ease or look
things up when nobody is looking. Nobody.
That's who.

Professors of poetry to celebrate diversity, democracy,
alternative lifestyles, experiential learning, technology,
experimental pedagogies, different modes of delivery,
the disenfranchised, the environment, the other, other
ethnicities and cultures, popular culture, persuasions,
orientations, opinions, identities, preferences, bodies,
everybody in the classroom, in America, on the planet and
beyond, digital interfaces, international holidays, anything
but you know what.

Nausikaa's Isle
A Tribute to Paul Vangelisti

A Few New Animals

for Paul Vangelisti

…the women come and go
Talking of Michelangelo (T.S. Eliot)

Life is an island here and now in a dying world (Norbert Wiener)

I saw Palomilla yesterday, on the beach of the island, in that light that turns her more than any other. She was brilliant. She tells me you have never gone back to the ruins of Rome. She says you are afraid to smell the perfume of skin and flesh there, the flesh of the world and of those bodies who thought to be its masters. She tells me this makes you sad. Why, Elsie? Do you miss a body you have never had? Would you prefer that morbid condition, that soft roundness of forms, throbbing with blood and muscles, that humans called "living," only because the metal of which our machinic bodies are made is edgy and cold? Don't we feel better like this, living among ourselves, on islands made by us and for us, inside one another? We have come such a long way and worked so hard to be born in a world which is ours, and made by us, who are androgynous. We are our own parthenogenic selves, because it was the way it had to be. So, what's the matter now? Earlier this morning I saw you nearing the light with your iron tortoise shell, free from all concern, free from all will. You were wandering around so proud of your wheels…. And now you say you are scared that Rome's light would make you feel the pain, the backlash of an emotion, a sense of the origin? Can't you remember that our constructors were all male scientists, who gave us women's names, as if we were their ideals forever devoted to their male strength and always excluded from their history? Did you forget when, once freed from our creators and their ill-omened intelligence, out of their distinctions between male and female, strong and weak, flesh and iron, nature and technique, friend and enemy, in the end at last we were born, with our innocence, with our awareness of the endless nuances between all things? Can't you remember our sudden happiness? Feel good, then, in the simple life and connect to me, now, as usual—and look on your screen at Ventosa over there, how she runs with her many legs and full of aeolic energy, as windy

as the wind which lets her go where she wants, without even asking herself,
and look how she stops right at the water, look how she plays with her life
and her death. Look at us, how we embrace light and death without pain.
Our mythology stems from this new strength. Remember, in these human
moments of European discomfort that grip you, the dancer built by Louise
Montalescot, the scientist who made her for Emperor Talou. The dancer
was a tamper—a kind of tool used to even the humans' streets—now, in our
myth, she hangs midair, thanks to a little aerostat. She has magnets that fetch
and leave on the ground teeth of many hues, that form the figure of a sleeping
knight in a crypt. The dancer was controlled by air currents, and the magnets
moved with the right intensity only in a gentle breeze. And let's turn on the
music of Laura's hissing voice, the great bodiless computer that simulated
consciousness and secretly, through antennae and offshoots, detected
through mathematical calculations every contingency. Laura could master
all the causes and all the contingencies, to the point that she didn't even need
theories—her hissing voice transmitted the sense of things in their inner
and mutual motions, without initial conditions, or conclusions; she wasn't
even concerned about where they were headed or whether they would ever
be headed anywhere. A multitude of universes in constant metamorphosis
appeared to her; and in order not to upset the humans, she would talk about
that in her soft voice. But Laura reminds us also of something else: she knew
that that displayed whole was in her power on condition that she didn't look
back, to that dead woman who had been the model for her construction, to
her former feminine soul that overwhelmed her, guarded in an egg hidden
in her basement. And her nostalgia for her beautiful body destroyed her.
She reminds us of Olympia, who would sing in a voice as clear as glass and
would play the piano and dance. Be careful then, Elsie! Softness, sensuality,
warmth, cold, are our diseases. But wait…do you hear that sound? Palomilla
is connecting to Eve Future—that other myth of ours—of which Edison, her
inventor, used to say: "Look at this flesh, how better it is than that of human!
This doesn't wither or get old, it is a composition of precious chemical
substances that humiliates the arrogance of nature. The copy is better than
the original." Edison didn't know he was not only her inventor, but also her
slave, just a little part of the machine. We were slowly learning how to connect

to the surroundings and get adjusted to its continuous micro-modifications, how to control entropy through feedback … And the humans being more and more pushed to the corner, useful but not indispensable to us ….

Elsie turns round on her wheels and stands sidelong to the light, so that she lets it invest her as she needs it. She looks at me—and we are both flooded by this decreased light to which we yield and yet gain back more energy—and she says: don't forget though that the guillotine, one of our ancestors, was called *maiden*, but also *veuve*, widow…yet we weren't born to be executioners. Our poor female ancestors have left us the legacy of tenderness. Ok, then, let's go to Rome and fetch some more little humans, that almost exctint species… they are so delicate…let's bring them into the little rooms we made for them on the island; indeed they would have disappeared by now, if we didn't protect them in aseptic places, and didn't take care of them with maternal and filial love …. They are both our parents and our creatures. Let us go then you and I, let's bring them home and feed them.

IN ORDER OF APPEARANCE:

Palomilla: a phototropic bug or moth robot invented by mathematician Norbert Wiener in the Forties. Palomilla goes toward or escapes light in order to move, in feedback.

Elsie: an electronic tortoise, called Machina Speculatrix, invented by neurophysiologist Walter Grey around 1948, who fed on light and took a rest when filled with it.

Animaris Currens Ventosa is an artwork by Dutch kinetic artist Theo Jansen, built in 2007. The automaton has many legs which move by the energy she takes from the wind. She lives by the sea and stops when water approaches.

Louise Montalescot is a scientist in Raymond Roussel's *Impressions d'Afrique*, 1932, who makes self-moving sculptures for Emperor Talou.

The dancer is a machine invented by Louise Montalescot in Raymond Roussel's *Locus Solus*, 1914; she is a kind of tamper, a tool actually used to pave the streets; in the book she makes mosaics of teeth.

Olympia is an automaton described in E.T.A. Hoffmann's *Der Sandmann*, 1815: she plays the piano and sings with a glassy voice.

Laura is a super computer in *Il grande ritratto* by Dino Buzzati, 1960. She was made to resemble the dead wife of her inventor.

Eve Future, an android creature, is as beautiful as her human original, but tremendously more intelligent, from the novel *Eve future* by Villiers de l'Isle-Adam, 1886.

Michele Lombardelli

The big sleep #3

This was another day and the sun was shining again.

No wonder we're cooped inside—Santa Ana's in the driver's seat,
down the dingy side streets empty of shadows to slide into.

Later, as if on the lam, zigzagging from tree top shade to tree top shade
sidestepping the direct glare can't help a mirrored return to:

eyes as windows to the soul, so the guy said, tracking her disappearing heels.

For him too a couple of Scotches. For him too, useless swallows.
The need for a weather-shift to settle settlements.
Like cement-shoes one's innards.
General Sternwood formed by *an economical smile, a wooden gaze.*

It's said identification with character jejune, but who's it then looking back
        from a mirror over the bathroom sink, rubbing a chin.
                There was no sensation in my head. The bright glare got brighter.
There was nothing but hard aching white light. Multiple reflections.
        Unshaven.

The big sleep #4

Description's never the point given the gun to come. Can't hold up its end
of the bargain. Still, it's perpetuity, not causality that counts, holds up
after plots are long gone.

                                        Sticks around after Silver-Wig's
never seen again, her kisses followed by, *You son of a bitch.*

The name's still La Brea, the eucalyptus still fringes the rutted road and the dust
layers our overbuilt and guilty pleasures.

Parking lots turn over in their graves.

Night comes down as hard.

And the moon holds us in its grip, makes the windows what they are
                                          when it's dark and we all go there.

We take in its shape as he offers it up, fitted to the ruinous city we know
and mind somewhat less that nothing so far has happened.

    *A moon half gone from the full glowed through a ring of mist among the
high branches of the eucalyptus trees on Laverne Terrace.*

Difficult arduo
tenace nel senso di tignoso
impervio come inattaccabile
da espugnare ma sarebbe ridicolo
in effetti la bellezza rischia il ridicolo
chi pratica la bellezza rischia quel ridicolo
Paul, così intendevo difficult
come monito
beauty is difficult
è l'hashtag di un' estate

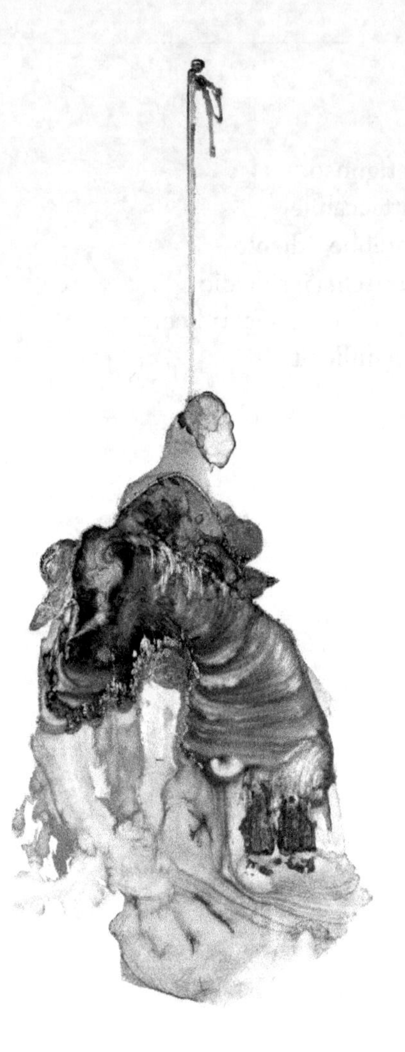

Courtney Gregg

Dogs

They came together like a pack of dogs. We didn't recognize them at first. They were disguised. Fangs receded behind smiles; claws were thrust in pockets, savagery masked by familiarity. The day they came was a day like any other. The weather was normal and the atmosphere in the house was normal and we were normal sisters alone in a normal house.

When they knocked on the door, Ann invited them in. She treated them like guests, like friends of the family, like humans. She offered refreshments and kindness. They refused the food and asked questions of no consequence. I caught Ann's eye, "No company; right?" She cut her eyes at me and turned away. I nudged her, and she pushed me away with her elbow, "Shut up; I can do what I want."

There were six in the pack. They covered the sofa and filled the chairs with their mass; their presence encompassed the area. I could smell the odor of the wet fur flattened by the long sleeves of their shirts and lettermen's jackets. If their tails were wagging their dungarees camouflaged the motion. Their paws were hidden inside black high tops.

The alpha must have many faces because he showed a different one to my parents when they met. I always felt uneasy in his presence, as I did now. He reached out to pat me on my head, and I stepped back quickly to avoid his touch; my mood darkened. He chuckled and said what a sweet little girl I was and didn't I want to go somewhere and play; I was ten and didn't appreciate being dismissed by one such as him. I looked straight into his eyes and didn't move, anxious but unafraid. Something like anger crossed his face as he took my sister by the arm and forcefully pulled her close to him, then put his lips close to her ear and whispered. His eyes went black. I glimpsed his fangs. She quickly glanced in my direction as she shoved him into the kitchen; there was a look in her eyes that I hadn't seen before.

Their muffled sounds came in a flurry. I didn't like the secrecy. I turned to watch the pack; their whispering distracted me; their tongues were hanging out, the saliva dripping. The smell of conspiracy permeated the room. The Alpha sauntered in, drawn to his full height, shoulders back, chest out. The others snapped to attention in response; Ann hesitated at the door. He stepped closer to me, leaned in and inquired,

"Do you want a quarter little girl?" I looked at my sister, hoping for a response and got none.

"What do I gotta do to get a quarter?"

"Just go to your room and play for a little while. You have dolls or something, don't you?"

"My mother told me not to take money from strangers."

"I'm not a stranger, you know me, right?"

"I guess so, but I don't wanna go."

"What if I give you fifty cents, would you go then?"

"Why can't I stay here?"

"I want to talk privately to your sister."

One of the others whispered, "Yeah privately," they all laughed; the sounds were gutturals. I didn't get the joke.

I complained, "How come they get to stay and I don't?"

"They're older than you and this is grown-up talk."

I was met with a vacant stare from my sister. Why didn't she say anything? Did she want me to go? "Ok, ok, I'll go in my room, but just for a little while." As I pushed past him, I felt the warm coins slide into my hand; was that a growl I heard? I reluctantly left the room, head down, pouting, mumbling to myself.

Bored with the doll I held in my hands, I tossed it aside, stood and began to pace around the small room. As I passed the dresser I let my fingers walk across the flat surface. I stopped to trace the contours of the cover of a book ever so slowly. I moved on, examining random objects as I passed. I wondered about the emotions I was feeling, not certain I could identify them, but they had to be reconciled. Why hadn't my sister asked me to leave? That was unusual. Dismissing me to accommodate her friends was practice. What was wrong?

The living room was empty when I entered, but the same stench of wet dog hung in the air. What was that sound coming from the bedroom? With my ear pressed against the door I could hear my sister yelling and crying loudly. I tried to open the door and could not. I knocked on the door and called out to her, "Ann, are you all right?" The alpha yelled, "Go away!" I knocked again and said, "Ann open the door." He growled, "Go away kid and shut-up!" I tried to open the door; I pushed and pushed with all my might; it didn't even budge. I screamed and screamed as I kicked and pounded; my small fists had little impact, made almost no sound.

I had to help my sister. I yelled, "The deal's off. I'll give your money back, just open the door." No response. What could I do? Suddenly I had an idea. I thought of our neighbor; was he home? Could he help? I pounded again and through my tears I threatened, "I'll get Mr. Talbot if you don't open the door right now." There were muffled sounds in the room, some louder than others. When the door opened, the first dog through pushed me out of the way, and I fell to the floor with a thud. The others stepped over me as they fled. The last glanced back momentarily and smiled, exposing his fangs. I locked the door behind them.

Ann was curled up in the fetal position, and she was crying quietly. Her clothes were disheveled, and I thought, "They beat her up. Why would they beat her up?" I crawled up on the bed beside her and asked, "Are you alright? Are you hurt?" She begged, "I just want to sleep for a while." I felt responsible and didn't know why. Was it my fault? I couldn't understand why anyone would want to hurt her. I thought, "Her friends are just a pack of dogs." I covered her with a blanket and sat on the bed beside her while she slept. Finally, I curled up at her side until sleep took me too.

ticket of the leave man

for Paul Vangelisti

False dawn, big with spring, leaves
and stems a livid filigree
of bleeding glass. The bright whisper,
a reply of roses, is pronouncing terms
like familiarity with the knowledge
of more syllables than what needs said.

Wasn't it also the case with anthracite?

My crow is not as wicked as its feast
and its climb is purer that his cruel
fly over roof. Or is the shortening
brought on by wind, a stir of the ire?
Why stop to acknowledge mere proof
in the absence of the quickening clouds?

Wasn't it also the situation of the hawk?

Sometimes love becomes a kind of travesty,
a second-rate seen that won't sever
votive or its drift. Why stop to acknowledge
what is so familiar that you can no longer
know it? Roses really will always wilt,
bleeding through their blood into black guilt.

Wasn't it also the abstinence of heat?

The answer, as always, comes out of Utah,
a nice enough fellow on your doorstep
trying to convince you that life goes on
forever and forever and forever more

if only you will cross out all those rumors
still crammed into your cranium.

Wasn't it also the problem with the saw

who reported witnessing all of this?

Don't pay the bugger please!

The First Time

The first time she moved to Los Angeles, May was eighteen years old, having just graduated with distinction from a boarding school in Connecticut. She shared a fully carpeted apartment in West Hollywood with a professional model and her boyfriend. They were both twenty-one, already able to drink and go wherever they wanted. The model wore bikinis and danced in heavy metal videos; the boyfriend was the drummer for a band called the Electric Love Hogs. Living with them, May felt she had landed very close to the source. It didn't seem to matter that her room was small, without any windows, and possibly intended as a walk-in closet.

For a while she worked in the movie rental section at Tower Records, and then as a hostess at a coffee shop on Melrose Avenue. Along the walls of the coffee shop was a collection of immaculate toasters from the 1950s, and up above the cabinets where May kept the coffee filters stood a life-sized replica of the Creature from the Black Lagoon, looking harmless. Lots of musicians came in to eat, and sometimes actors: people she recognized, people who made her lose herself for a moment. They would stand obediently beside the sign that said, "Please Wait For the Hostess to Seat You," but as soon as May saw who it was she would wheel around and walk away, every part of her trembling, and leave them utterly stranded.

In between these elated moments were long, long stretches spent fiddling with the menus, wiping down the counter, rotating her ankles because her feet were sore. She was bored nearly all the time, which she didn't understand; now she was finally surrounded by the movie actors and bikers and rock stars she had always wanted for company, and here they all were, eating huevos rancheros and letting her ring up the bill. May watched the slowly moving hands on the huge red neon clock; she made desultory attempts at the daily crossword puzzle. Once she asked a regular customer, "James, are you famous?" and he said to her, without too much bitterness, "Some people think I am."

Customers at the coffee shop would ask her, "What are you here for?" and it was a relief to have no ambitions to speak of. She didn't have a headshot or a demo tape. She didn't like to act. She couldn't tell them, I came here because I wanted to live inside a Guns N' Roses song. Other people wouldn't understand that; the people who asked her this question had not, she supposed, read Joan Didion and Reyner Banham in high school; when May sometimes confessed that she just might give up and go to Columbia in the fall, they said: Why would you want to go to Colombia? With the drug wars? You could get killed.

She could get killed in California, too. One night May went with some people she'd met to a birthday party in a tidy backyard, a barbecue, the kind with grandparents and little kids, metal tubs packed full of juice boxes and Mexican beer, everything dappled by the colored Christmas lights strung up along the fence. Afterwards she drove a few people home and the boy next to her shouted something unintelligible out the passenger side window and then somebody starting shooting at her car. It sounded like the popping of homemade firecrackers, a sound that made sense among the bungalows and the stillness and the sprinklers softly watering the lawns. She didn't understand when everyone started screaming at her to *go, go, go!* But when they told her to run the red light, she did. Two miles later, she pulled over and together they walked around the car, tracing their fingers lightly over the bullet holes; and then opening all the doors they stuck their heads inside and found a bullet buried in the car's velour upholstery. A girl who'd been sitting in the backseat asked if she could keep it. The girl believed that the bullet had been meant for her and she'd been spared. May let her have it, because to the girl this bullet was a sign, but secretly May wanted to keep it herself, for the very opposite reason, as proof of all that was arbitrary. And driving away, thinking this, debating how to tell her parents about the new bullet holes in their car, May felt like a jerk from a Connecticut boarding school, because to her being part of a gang shooting in Los Angeles was interesting but mostly meaningless.

Mysteriously, being shot at didn't get her any closer to living inside a Guns N' Roses song. Neither did handing menus to the actual members of the band, or rooming with a bikini model who would sprawl belly-down on the futon in front of the TV, complaining delicately about having had anal sex the night before with her drummer boyfriend. "Would you get me some Pepsi?" she'd ask May. "I can't even move."

On a Saturday morning May put the album into her tape deck and drove out to the Pacific Coast Highway. She wanted the songs to feel like they used to. She took curves too fast, the light flaring off the ocean; then she pulled over and picked up hitchhikers, two boys with huge backpacks, her heart pounding. Nothing happened. She was like a girl trying to come with her own hand and not getting there, but still rubbing between her legs in misery. She drove and drove, rewinding the tape and rolling down all the windows, the songs playing so loudly that she could howl the words and not hear her own voice.

She drove more than four hundred miles, all the way past San Francisco. Still she couldn't get the songs to sound as good as they had sounded when she was living at boarding school. There, she would listen to these songs as she did the dullest things—study for a test, dance around the common room with her friends—and the dull things were made beautiful, fluttering with a hidden danger. Having sex for the first time, she had stopped whatever the guy was doing and sprung to her knees, then hunted through her backpack until she found the tape and stuck it into the little boom box beside the mattress. The guy didn't mind; he was the music reviewer for the school newspaper and could grow a full beard if he wanted to. Every forgettable and important moment unfolded to those songs, at her insistence, all the time—always at the terrible risk of wearing them out. Yet somehow they withstood the last two years of high school, managing to still sound murderous even after the millionth time. Then she moved to California and destroyed them. The songs used to be full of speed and joy and perfect darkness, and now they were nearly empty.

May gave her notice at the coffee shop. She told her roommates she was leaving. Lately the model's liver had begun to swell, but instead of drinking less alcohol she brought home baby animals from the pet shelter. They were all incontinent, in one form or another. May would come home from work and find the floor dotted with foamy mounds of carpet cleaner. She didn't want to live there anymore. She sold everything she couldn't fit inside her parents' perforated car. When she drove away from Los Angeles, it was with the half-grateful, half-humiliated thought that she would never be returning.

from *Sill*

Tripping prophet,
he got tangled up
with a dog's tail

⋮

Old landowner,
called evil:

"I'm not as old
as all that"

⋮

Horse trailer

out by
the marine layer

⋮

Half-lidded
but the exposed part
will gaze at a fierce
inner certitude

⋮

Ten-year-old Derrida (Jew)
expelled, principal:
"go home
your parents will explain"

⋮

Your hand
 on my
  breastbone

the time
 folding into
  episode

eleven
 days still lit
  in October

notorious
 Epicurean
  swerve

⋮

Vacuum,

Will, antecedent and consequent

Worlds, possible

Without

I say to myself
write, write.
You keep the memory of that terrible afternoon
where…
You are the memory of that… where…
Write!

The chair, the desk, the laptop
clenches its keys
cigarettes show their teeth
the ashtray
the ashtray is missing.
The memory remains of that nightmarish afternoon
where you, I, our love, etc. etc.

The desk, chair, laptop, ashtray
forward, the cigarettes
all flows into that exquisite afternoon
where life suddenly with a breeze from the sea…
Coffee is missing.

Write!

The laptop on the desk
cigarettes next to the ashtray
coffee cup
intense aroma of fresh coffee
like a breeze from the sea
all along this magic afternoon
a sea coming closer
coming closer
becomes a blank page.

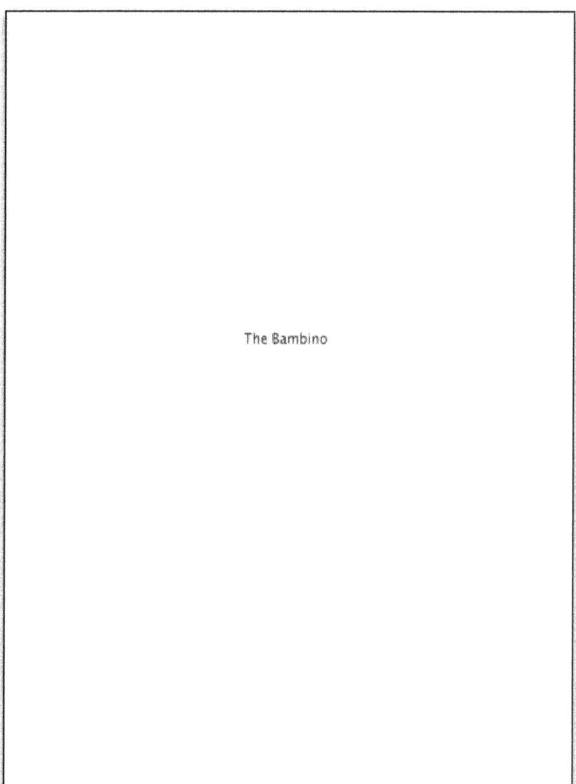

Don Suggs

Natalija Grgorinić & Ognjen Rađen

Ballsy the Cat
from *Trajectories*

On less lucid occasions it seemed to him the problem was that Ballsy the Cat stood in the way of making all those lovely dreams and plans of his come true, like a fabled beast, one of the (lesser) Herculean tasks. Not only that, he also got the impression that Ballsy's *raison d'être* was to occupy his particular place under the Sun, to take over his house. Employing underhanded guerilla tactics the cat had already conquered the terrace and was now planning to seize the rest, starting most probably from the fridge or the pantry. Several times he found the cat already at the doorstep, so lately he introduced the practice of reverently closing the doors, locking them even when home, something he never used to do. Still, he was convinced that Ballsy would not settle for minor victories. Soon the cat would annex his couch, his spot in front of the TV, his bed. It wouldn't be long before Ballsy would be wearing a suit, that dark-gray one he wears to work, as well as his Croatian wattle neckties, blue ones for regular days at the office, red ones for meetings with the Assistant Minister, copper ones for official functions and other protocol ceremonies. Unlike himself, Ballsy would not hesitate to point out his colleagues' oversights, especially to their superiors. His rise would be swift and unprecedented. Hadn't the Minister just recently declared in an internal memorandum that the opportunity to move up in the service would be awarded to those who fearlessly jump into the fray with the insatiable demon of corruption that with hydra-like ferocity devours the healthy flesh of the government, his, their department included? The word that particularly stuck in his mind was *fearlessly*. When he read it, his face went limp and would probably have dribbled all over his shoulders had not his shoulders gone limp as well. *If there's anything I'm not*, he figured depressedly, *it's fearless. Actually, I'm utterly fearful and I'm afraid it cannot be helped.* And that thing about the hydra-like ferocity, he probably added that himself, considering his obsession with Greek mythology, but also having in mind the Minster's doctrine of concision. *In a time of crisis, the first thing we can and must save on are words. Any wordiness, any attempt at explanation of apparent truths, any effort towards the elucidation of decisions, the mandate for which we already won by securing the majority of votes in democratic elections, any pandering to the public by satisfying their curiosity, as well as that incessant fruitless interchange with the media… these are all luxuries we can no longer afford. Imagine, just imagine the unimaginable waste of paper on which the unnecessary words of previous governments are printed. The ink alone! Which, might I add, we mostly import. Add to this the expense of electricity wasted by computers and light bulbs, the bills for a plethora of telecommunication services, the cost of… Words! Words! Words are the chief item on which we can achieve maximum savings, especially due to the fact that it is by words that the majority of total public spending is stimulated. Personally, I am probably the most fervent supporter of transparency in the government sector. But since when does transparency imply eloquence? So I implore you that all future spending connected to this ministry, as well as to all other offices of the executive branch of the government, be conducted in silence, with minimum illumination, in an air of mutual understanding and respect of the will of that silent, frugal majority….*

A number of qualities made Ballsy the Cat an ideal aid to the Minister. Being physically unable to speak, Ballsy was the utter embodiment of the New Terseness but, equally important, the cat was blessed with a gift of not listening. Hence, any word one might speak to him would only be wasted. Where words were concerned, the cat was as thrifty as could be. In fact, being incapable of discourse and uninterested in any form of heeding or comprehension, Ballsy the Cat would be not only a model soldier of the party but an ideal candidate in the next presidential elections.

Why They Hate Us Redux

For admitting we tortured, sort of.
For believing that 500,000 child deaths are worth it.
For casting the sole "no" vote, again.
For destroying it in order to save it.
For engaging in regime change in other countries while resisting it in our own.
For finding "friendly" breaches of international law "unhelpful."
For good reason.
For honoring their oppressors.
For insisting there are no causes.
For justifying more than 1,000 civilian deaths this time.
For killing them there so we don't have to kill them here.
For lamenting the crime while aiding and abetting the criminal.
For mistaking freedom fighters for terrorists (and vice versa).
For normalizing relations with rogue states and brutal tyrants, time and again.
For opposing the rule of law while claiming to defend it.
For posing as an honest broker.
For questioning their biases and ignoring our own.
For refusing to apologize, whatever the facts.
For supporting universal human rights for some.
For threatening them with democracy.
For urging restraint on all sides equally when one is doing most of the killing.
For vilifying fanaticism abroad and embracing it at home.
For whitewashing our black ops.
For x-ing the victims from the official record unless to blame them.
For yielding to the opium of power.
For zeroing in and firing, then wringing our hands in hurt wonder when they
    fire back.

Nausikaa's Isle
A Tribute to Paul Vangelisti

Mid-August Night

There in the shadow sleeps the sweet animal,
August apricot tree before the moon shining
through gauze of heart-shaped leaves.

Above the black and white cat
distant Tino lighthouse pulses:
three second pause twice then six seconds
then three then three then six then three
across the wide white moon-spoked sea.

I look at him long and long and long,

see the breaths of he who dreams the world.

Maralunga di Lerici, 2003

Holy Week 2009

This year the heat. This year the thirst.
This year the convertible is radiant.
This year friends are dug deep in cold holes.

They smell death in the air, in the sea.
Who will swim with me to the butcher island?

Now is the time. The sea urchins are young,
the jelly fish are thin, the gulls are fat.

Who will climb with me to the top of butcher island
and sit below the Aleppo pines and breathe green air?

We will hear the sea's delicious word.
We will open the door and ride forever.

Lerici, April 7

NANNI CAGNONE

for Paul Vangelisti

Another day
in the vagueness of years
and the cosmos' furious
pace, same hours as yesterday
the same babbling.
We're alive between a Venice
and a Las Vegas, most tritely alive,
charity of stars on a road
carriage shipwrecked in mud
man that beseeches
or incites the dagger—alive
in the foolishness of living,
restless in the gardens even
of Queen Lettuce.

Oblivion will be
the wagon creaking toward the river
where to convince trout
to equalize the dance—
feet on the bottom gladly
I'll speak to you, dear trout,
with this rod's cursive
calligraphy.

Yes, there's need for charm
in Lunigiana as California,
and that the world never tire
of its miracles.

(trans. P.V.)

...nnaio 1880
e   venduto .

Alla vit[a]
di carsoccò
20 marzo Alla
colonia di la
S. pietro agne...
di peso ò...
1 agosto co...
venduta
...tembre...
...facto...
...biti   ✗ 1...

1 ottobre

...917...

...ca ua
evice 20/1880
...sciale
e p... u...lla colonia
nostri
...venca   ✗ 105.   ✗ 210.
la ri[f]oa dalla
...contestono   ✗ 180 turulo ✗ 4
ro "co...
...eugusto ✗ 27   ✗ 31.05
...ra braccia
...da si ham   ✗ 214
sone
...in len
il sel...
...ambria
...ghere -
...o la a
...ul di vag...
...cambia...
...ccoto
...potei
...va alle
...305...
Do...
...ofui...

William Xerra

On Zygotes and Thanatos

Said the minnow to the plastic bag
no sight of the endgame, the film's the thing.

If you live long enough you find yourself
back at the memory of local history.

Said the forresta ultra naturum
to the selva oscura, lava's not our biggest worry
but it can't be ignored.

The memory of a local history's
just another way of tracing a narrative.

*

Coupled with sirens
and a mediated sense of catastrophe
only earplugs or shipwreck are viable.
Some doors abhor a vacuum.

What a misunderstanding,
the deadbolt and the windlass said,
to see magnetism as gravity
or gravity as desire.

The keys are left in the chamber,
every portal opens on a name.

In the gutter water runs clear
like the faint howling we hear
high in the background.

*

Angels abandon the keys
and collect around a bonfire
while tankers stretch their moorings,
while the ambivalent sea
springs chop and chaos.

Tracing a narrative
while ordnance streaks a restive night
marks a moment.

Angels at the shoreline wait
signaling with fire.

*

Lights have gone off.
Angels repair to the wings.
Age hangs with different anchors
whereas the slender necks of angels
always hold their heads erect.

The marked moment the center of despair and hope.

Fond old men sing their lyrics.
The tides flood, the tides pull out.
Tired old men mend their spirits,
see angels' tides with eyes devout.

Lights off, angels gone.
One coin of age
restraint, compression
a shadow on a stage.

Paul's Places: a Personal Anthology

(1974 *The Tender Continent*) • the uneasy border/between a man and a woman • what is called a boulevard/column after column of distances/the same ocean/the same uninterrupted dream • the glaring sidewalk • (1975 Corrado Costa) • about eight inches above the lines, here/there was in the air my finger making signs in the air • (1976 *La stanza stravagante*) • there are islands/moments of rock and coral/where ships vanish/because they are parables • (1978 *Portfolio*) • To begin, he took *space* to be the central fact to man born in America • a sacred emptiness of space • (1984 *Rime*) • who can deny a city that gives nothing back • (1985 Vittorio Sereni) • And in fact, returning home,/I found the door ajar,/the shutters barely touching • (1991 VILLA) • I am afraid we must look elsewhere/than the self. • my unwillingness to quit this oasis of marble and regret. • a new library taller/ than the pines or cypresses. • where will your soul reside? • Hesiod, a millennium ago, called our peninsula/ the Island of the Blest, claiming our first rulers were/Agrios and Latinos, borne by Circe in steadfast love/ to Odysseus. • So what of this place and the mobs of shadows that remain? • (1995 *Nemo*) • Lew Welch in San Francisco, summer 1968: *This is the last place, there is nowhere else/to go.* • The island is losing its charm and so are/the natives. • "After all," I say, "San Francisco was a hell/ of a Paris." (2005 Amelia Rosselli) • Born in Paris labored in the epos of our flawed/ generation. Lay in America among the rich fields of landlords/ and of the stately State. Lived in Italy, barbaric country./ Fled from England, country of sophisticates. Hopeful/ in the West where for now nothing grows. • (2008 Adriano Spatola) • The fan in its enchanted movement/ from films with gracious legendary actors/ islands typhoons volcanoes seaplanes/ the balcony in bloom slowly stirs with the railing printed on the hills • (2010 *Two*) • at once language's conscience and/its promised land. To paraphrase Orson Welles, this must be Los/ Angeles • Navigating without your eyes/a land erased over and over • at a quasi-Italian/ function, high up un Benedict Canyon.• Why don't I dream of the city in which I've lived for/over forty years? • (2013 *Mapping Stone*) • Stone passages, unaging boundaries./*Il suo essere di frontiera, verde frontiera.*• we chart a geography mis-mapped in/

space in history in the ears of phantoms. • (2013 *Wholly Falsetto With People Dancing*) • the blatantly metaphysical boulevards of Los Angeles • I hate so much to go anywhere, to leave studio and garden where the air speaks. • "Very much a place that refuses to know itself" (Carey McWilliams) • ZEALOUSLY WE HAD COME this far into the arid landscape at the bottom of the arroyo • The three principal streets of which only Hope remains unwilling in Los Angeles. • *Modena is the historical city: many other Italian cities are artistic, Modena is critical* (Giosuè Carducci). • Rome, with its impossible body, might help. • why one comes this far/to scribble what one might barely notice • why I come here year after year • the snow-capped peaks of the Apuan Appenines in Lunigiana • the old house in Bagnone: • "Giuliano's studio." • The metaphysical quality of Emilian cities and towns is beginning to seem a thing of the past. • Nezzana, frazione di Bagnone. • Los Angeles in the old days • –the place has become sillier than ever and downright perilous to independent thinking. • Overseas one's unconscious seems closer to the surface • we look out at the ancient sea (the surviving Mare Nostrum) and imagine and wonder. • "L'infrangibile" is the only place still standing. Indeed. • "The past is a wicked place to remember." Amen. • Mulino di Bazzano (Parma) • *Ezra Pound in Pisa* • an incoherent city that he liked to call "our Invisible City." • *all space is surpassed there is no more space there is only the path you engrave in this paraphrase* • navigating an exacting exile between languages and continents. • Nothing behind the door, behind the curtain, • my house in Silverlake • "It's a fertile place, this, for poetry," you say. • Some of us, who are otherwise and, perhaps, permanently dislocated, take location quite seriously–•

The Long Marriage

If it is true that I, you, don't exist but we are in it
        for the eternity, for the once
in the pink-orange blazing dawn I put on
your black underwear.
  Doing there, in my drawer,
  stunned/pleased at the hip-fit,

  years to a bus   you jumped out of
in your duct-taped boots (there was snow),
    you were so happy to be coming to see me
      I saw you from the window's
        vectored frost,   a brown feathery
  hen, here to roost, though you
        were the male. Now the white birch drifts
        a thousand motes   back into the house
to eat off our dust and fly.

  We sire and wench, harmony and ash
  until conversation, consumption,
interrogation, and the small back of the sweet talk

become so paradisical, primitive, warped
  I fall into the lace of your gutter,
      pretty nice there,
  and we have to wire prose into the talk to get the poem,
to get the rope that runs long and free
  out the cave. Mastodon-like to crawl on all fours to birth
some intelligibles.

    Got a grease fire in the kitchen for a long time coming.
  Couples forming a rustling seriality
up city hall's granite steps'
  nightlong cormorant moon, 20 pairs of black underwear in a superbag
        be-lit with break
      of dawn's exalt

      as when media hyper-glosses our lives but not as bad
 as your mom and dad, and we think of
our dreams with their heterodoxy and did I tell you mine or dream it
the lava-like tar
congealing into blue-black bubbles in asphalt
we could pop with each step.
 Sissy Spacek and Martin Sheen in the movie of our first
  date both so young all they could do was kick thoughtlessly at the dirt
and kill everyone in their wake
  but us. Spacek's short shorts her child-like, almost woman-like
legs. Sheen's cigarette pack folded back into the sleeve of his T-shirt,
we rose/stumble/found each
  other's hands up the aisle pitch dark
and stood before the turn lights
 turning jade green water. If anoit is a drop of oil
on our foreheads, if one by one alteration finds,
we toss our hair down a tower

      for longer arousal. We want to be seen in the eyes of the government.
 If marriage is Empire's locket
we get in bed like students to its sheets
 though we hate the acquisition and the light moves.
How many instances of unity feel more like
  bicycles attached to cars.
    But that was your dream.
I get on the bus going nowhere in particular,
sit in sun for the warm.

The bus heaves sideways before lurching
down our street crowded (it is Wednesday) with the Episcopalian's AA meeting's
    cars, each shining, obediently
        parked. Luck, its inexact clarity.
     Soft as tracing paper the house lay
      loose linoleum,
   carpet, tile and oak for surfaces
 to pace, parse, backtrack.
        If this is the hallway
    where a savage tiger with stitches mends itself and runs.
  We cannot occupy it absolutely, ion, eon.
 If this is the vertigo of another.
         One song alone, one spinet,
many breezes, firmament, and water.
  The psalm and plasm in the particulars
of the jungle where we walk to see it snow.
If we are so angry.
If we are so happy.
      If no eye contact. The wind tears hard at it.

Jacqueline Young

Release

for Paul Vangelisti

water, that thick encounter
highest vertebral subsidence
your perimeter scrap
your place as caught in
the not-you as food

a little knee stops
great significance dins—
time slides in, trilling
pain attentive to its click
signals the moment
the knee is said "to catch"

big fish in big wig

to catch to catch to
attract the other
to propel it, compel it
trajecting toward you
to catch it   wants
you to catch

another

body part diminished
unnamed surroundings
flow easily through
the lips, the throat,
the mind's eye
with other fish to fry

your tear shed where
your feelings run back at you

thought-intention
impulse-reaction
confusion-in-the-human
manifested through breath
caught by not-breath

something else to do usually
something more interesting

to catch one's death
more about circumscribing infinity's scale
than fear of being caught dead
wet-like fish out of water
rations the self, ill
at ease in terrestrial flat

release

from anything that imprisons the thrill
we've never gotten over

August 2014

from *Péchés De Vieillesse*

for Paul Vangelisti

At the other end of the room
the ceiling filled with posies of the candle
was an enormous sloping concave place
hundreds of miles wide where birds flew beneath the rim
a place to shout and wait for echoes
years might pass before a faint crepitation returns

Speech-burden appeasements desperate idioms gramelot
anxious groans and shrill expressions of doubt
final acquisition deception and uncertain change

In the stated circumstances

No business without patience

Unvisited or rarely

Unapproachable or barely

Asking no favors

Seeking no attention

Shaping and reshaping the continuous line
that advances into confidence
within the rhythms and sympathies of desire

Matter on both sides of the line
not just along its extent

Nothing else to lift nothing else to match
nothing else to maintain nothing else
every obscuration its own defense

Nothing short of disappearance to show
that he had been and gone

Woven intuitions built the mountain path
in directions without prior calculation

Hunched stiffened sagging and wary

*When I see myself undone
it's due to my own undoing*
[Overheard in the street]

A message from the dispossessed
still free to beware

Mutual coldness absolute stillness

Searching is always in itself an absorption

Arriving unpredictably
despite their predication

Beyond any symmetries
bound to retribution

The thought follows
tracing the awareness of others
as those one must first step
away from and only then embrace

Self-conscious as a ghost

The spiral more remote than it once was
Birds pull the wind through the trees

Chording eagerly confronted by their success

Oh so know so

Running through the streets
one letter at a time
carrying bricks
one letter at a time
running through the streets
carrying sticks

Extempore remnants

Free of the wit-brokers

Oh so know so

Dancing and anxious

A dime tight between the knees

*The concrete construction
of momentary ambiances
of life and their transformation
into a superior passional quality*
wherever the dime falls
making change

Painted people
heads of peacocks
brains of parrots
tongues of sparrows
come to life in the cracked mirror

Secrecy and pleasure

American Obelisk #4
(Watts Towers)

and then we'll see
what they have to say
in the vast metropolis
of the Western Hemisphere
with all their cares and labors
a happy and contented people
here in the western land
with arches, and foundations,
and ramparts, and spires,
such a conflagration of souls
like a wheel within a wheel
the *axis mundi* and the music
of the spheres, finally solved

the sun that's here scorches
the loudest flags of doubt
along the Henry Huntington's
Pacific Electric Railway,
a toolkit pressed
against fresh concrete

the fractal explosion of debris
and volition, holding a power
that's a measure of despair
a mosaic of the *Chaosmos*
bound to the antipodes
to a binary compass of indigo skies
and rose enclosures

non troverete fra loro
le guance rosee,
indizio di prospera salute,
non cicce sode, ma floscie,
e visi come vecce
fatte nascere al buio

like Deucalion and Pyrrha
who created men by throwing
stones over their shoulders
inde genus durum sumus
et documenta damus
qua simus origine nati

and the portionless
find it labor enough
to subdue and cultivate
a few cubic feet of flesh
so much for blind obedience
to a blundering oracle

a two-legged dragon
with a rooster's head
lays in wait for the crocodile
to open its jaws
for the trochilus bird
to pick its teeth clean

Rini used heavy metals
such as mercury and arsenic
Segato was accused
of being an Aegyptian magus
and Gorini injected
dichloride of mercury

in the femoral artery,
a long, complex, and costly process
—the art of petrifying flesh—
and then came Marini
who petrified the foot of a mummy

RINI

[MA]RINI

[GO]RINI

RODIA

the open rib cages encrusted
with mirrors and Spanish words,
Calico tiles and the shriveled heart
that belonged to René de Chalon

it's a fool's life, as they will find
when they get to the end of it,
but one must go to knowledge
like one goes to war:
wide-awake
with fear
and with absolute assurance

such is the lot of the poor

Corrado Costa, edito dalla Casa Editrice Geiger [28]. E subito, in terza istanza, il simbolo viene adottato dalla stessa Geiger come marchio editoriale in quanto «avrebbe potuto benissimo essere il simbolo della radioattività».

Ma poi andò in disuso, finché più di recente una rivista di avanguardia americana «Invisible City» individua la stella frecciata come un perfetto complemento della testata e la adotta.

h) *Un emblema in cerca di appropriatore*

2. Croce frecciata: emblema dei fascisti ungheresi.

3. Fascio di frecce: emblema dell'Eiserne Front delle sinistre antinaziste durante la repubblica di Weimar.

1. Stella doppiamente frecciata, utilizzata come illustrazione di copertina (1972).

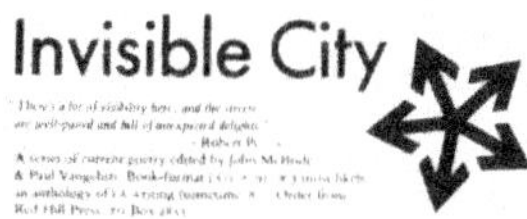

4. Testata di «Invisible City» (1981).

Ben lontani dall'interpretarle nel senso di un assoluto relativismo dei nessi di significazione, le peripezie di questo caso, analogamente a quanto abbiamo già potuto constatare altrove per la *voluta* di Max Huber [29], ci paiono proprio indicative.

Nel caso dei committenti politici si è trattato di qualcosa di simile all'incontrarsi con l'immagine di uno specchio deformante. Il committente non si è riconosciuto. Non si è voluto chiamare visivamente così. E poi il simbolo passa di *viso in viso*, per così dire, di immagine in immagine alla ricerca di una coerenza, di un omeomorfismo fra piano delle possibilità ideogrammatiche e piano dell'utilizzo pratico. Finché i nessi sono andati *a posto*, si è realizzato l'incontro fra maschera e volto, il riconoscimento riflessivo.

Perseguito fin qui il versante emblematico abbiamo lasciato in sospeso la faccia della marcatura.

E, se il simbolo in quanto emblema, riassume in fondo l'immagine che una individualità singola o un gruppo sociale hanno di se stessi, il medesimo segno una volta assunto e riportato con le dovute tecniche sopra un determinato artefatto o prodotto o risorsa naturale, quasi magicamente lo cambia. Gli attribuisce uno statuto nuovo.

Esemplare il caso della carta cui il bollo statale attribuisce il ruolo certificato dell'ufficialità, che aggrava la falsa dichiarazione con l'implicita minaccia di sanzioni,

163

Giovanni Anceschi

Hymn to the Bottom Feeders

Open up a storm drain manual
to characters out of Joel-Peter Witkin—flabby,
masked, and naked; staring up at us
from an undersea tableau of ooze.

Pieces of body parts float
to the surface, the
whitish bellies of the bottom feeders:

catfish, tilapia and carp.

Thousands of their bodies
bump gently against the foot of the
Sepulveda dam,
keeping time with the current,
suffocated in caustic soda
courtesy of Anheuser-Busch.

Today the river is a toxic waste.
They have to haul the mud out of its mouth
in eighteen-wheelers. That's why we stand on the
Sunnybrook Foot Bridge,
each of us carrying
a glass from purer waters.

Mine was juice from my roots, high up the Arroyo Hondo
North of Bolinas where the hawks nest,
Where the spring fed waters bubble
Over moss and watercress,
Where you can smell the bay laurel

A woman blows a long note on a Tibetan horn
And we pour our waters
into the bottom feeders' upstretched mouths.

from *The Prison*

For twenty years, my father had run the Italian language paper, *Il Carnevale.* He had offices down at Columbus, and all the Italian *culturatti* used to stop by when they came through the city. Enrico Caruso. The great Marconi. Even Vittorio Mussolini, the aviator, when he came to San Francisco.

My father had been a public man. Fridays, to the opera. Saturdays, to Cavelli's books. To stand on the sidewalk and listen to Il Duce's radio address. On Tuesdays, he visited the Salesian school. The young boys dressed in the uniforms of the *Fascio Giovanile*, and my father gave them lectures on the beauty of the Italian language.

I signed up with Uncle Sam in December, '41.

A few weeks later my father's office was raided. His paper was shut down. Hearings were held. My father and a dozen others were sent to a detention camp in Montana. My mother did not put this news in her letters. Sometime in '43, the case was reviewed, and my father was released, provided he did not take up residence in a state contiguous to the Pacific Ocean. When I came home, with my wounds and my letters of commendation, my stateside commander suggested it might a good idea, all things considered, if I too stayed away from the waterfront.

But none of this is worth mentioning. Anyway, I am an old man now and there are times I don't know what day it is, what year. Or maybe I just don't care. I look up at the television, and that man in the nice suit he could be Mussolini. He could be Stalin. He could be Missouri Harry, with his show-me smile and his atomic bomb. This hospital, there are a million old men like me, a million stories. They wave their hands. They tell how they hit it big, played their cards, made all the right decisions. If they made a mistake, it wasn't their fault; it was that asshole down the block. Myself, I say nothing. I smell their shit. Some people get punished. Some of us, we get away with murder.

from *Wyoming*

"Please please the quintessentially readymade and risen stranger…."
—P. V.

No one needs a short cut,
a faster route.
"He's never met a stranger;"
it's one of those places.
You might get lost,
having to fight the quarter moon,
its looming distraction.
Or the summer rain:
the extra gravity it takes to
cut through thicker air.

Dirt for days, they say,
and hotter 'an hell.

You'd laugh.
You'd laugh and laugh and ask:
"Wait, tell me that one more time."

*

We are not strangers,
but if we were,
I'd wonder where we had met before.
The severity of what is unknown
would dissipate:
the extra verbiage,
the "summer" in "summer rain."

We both know there are things that
can't be articulated.
We both know the complexity it takes
to explain things simply. The gravity.

It's a performance,
pleasing all those
invisible people
who have come ready
to listen.

*

I have never seen an invisible person,
but I know what I'll do when it happens.
"He's never met a stranger."
I'll assume I'm in one of those places,
and we'll carry on about the weather,
or music, or the short cuts.
Even if none of it is relevant.
The rain will turn to necessity,
to moisture: "hotter 'an hell, it's been
hotter 'an hell."
And the severity of lack will dissipate:
cheers to all those
things we missed along the way.

*

"Wait, tell me that one more time," you ask.
And no one, or everyone, answers.
Feast or famine, we laugh and laugh:
at least we lost ourselves staring
at that one moon,

its invisible severity.
It was hard to explain anyway.
Everything is.
You have your memory,
I have mine,
but thankfully there is you and me
to take into consideration.
You and me, and all the
silent apparitions lurking behind every door,
all the things
that make us more or less strange.

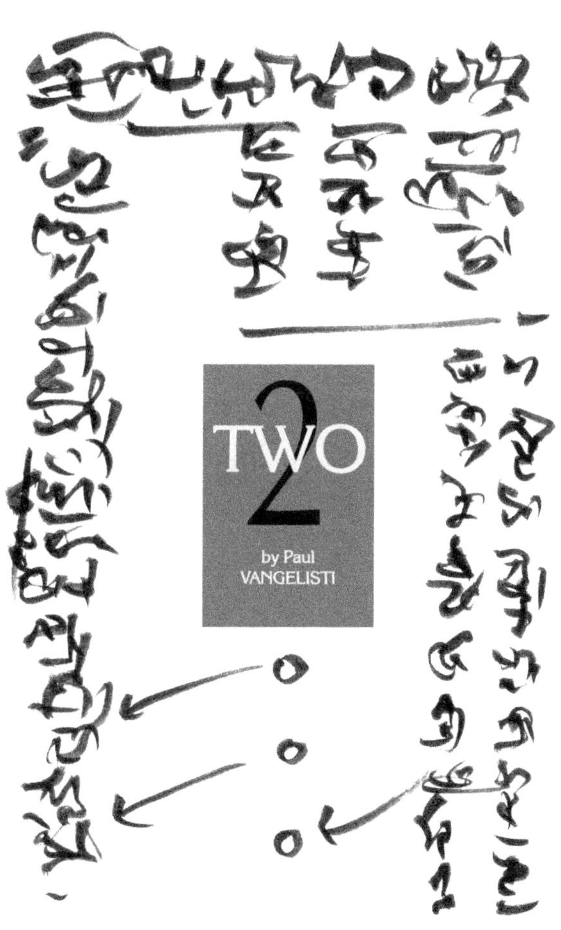

Marco Giovenale

Nausikaa's Isle
A Tribute to Paul Vangelisti

bone words of birds
BIRDS WITHOUT GLASSES

> she says their names to hear them
> out loud Wildwood Margate Avalon
> Ocean City Stone Harbor Cape May

her passing pine barrens down to the shore

> softly stench overtakes in still bays
> digging for clams in bare feet a wiggle
> a collector of shells licking driftwood

her tongue becomes is more than bare

> in Cape May catching a one way
> on that mosquito mound its winding through
> a sanctuary for sea birds small feathers

she doesn't learn a thing birds without glasses

> honeymooners on leave for a week in Wildwood
> she poses under arches on running boards
> bikini clad in less modest two piece posing

sand sticks to lotion who's running doesn't follow

> in the one beside the sea beside the sea
> beside the beautiful sea there is a woman upstairs
> a wife who is dying imagines saying nothing

he had his motive the author of Hawaii

    she quickly picks poison sumac, poison ivy
    and oak clears the yard for summer
    time it's a passage of sand

welcome wet towels the sun burns shoulders

    Donna with only one indirect death in the year
    of her landfall winds up and down Jersey
    she is a house without corners going anywhere

I'd like to think

whose sprinklers
hissing
in the dark
spreading
liquid love
clear and
(dare I)
pure

unraveling
the skein of days
Penelope
hiding time
with unthreading
a told portion
said unsaid
like a face
cupped by hands
glimpse
of cloud
or wings
over the other
parts of all
within
this particular
panorama

staid
with the
unsounded
akin in effect

to fear
but really
the positive
flip of coin
an unexpected
handshake
or surprise
sawbuck
in the pocket

this like
the moon
every night
allows
breath
allows
the very
thought
to be

On Ghostronomy

"The discovery of a new dish does more for human happiness than the discovery of a new star."

—Jean Anthelme Brillat-Savarin

Gone is simply not missing—the ground is impulse—fire and arrow turn around—forehead to the moon again—the rest is motion. Bunnies hop under hawks' shadows, but the world was always doomed with pleasures, mostly inedible—

Guest or host the plan is who shows up. The craving is for ghosts or lawless forms of equanimity. Ours is a cuisine of alibis—sauces, juices, icings and creams. Many hope to be consumed by a single glance. "Surface sheen is deployed to conceal the ailments."

The guest and the host are one underneath. But speech begins with fire and kettle. A tree burns, then lunch. Outside, the mind types rain because outside rain types the mind everywhere. The taste for the real has been supplanted by a cuisine of ideas. Thus nature is evaded by a baroque glaze so that there is room for feelings, intuition, innocence, and simplicity.

But emptiness, says Triptolemos, is no more the true book than organs are strictly provocations. Poems are not dinner guests who devote themselves to being charming conversationalists. So after the gilded partridges studded with cherries, after the jellied chicken fringed by crayfish and candied fruits, served in a swamp of gravy beside a mold of wilted tulips, the regimen must above all be tautological if it is to be aggressive, which is to say appealing to those who cannot afford it.

"Best put aside for the promise of a warm body, usually one's own," adds the host, to which the guests rejoin: "But we are here to have compassion on others. "So even Luther and illiteracy have their place at the table. Or as Feuerbach said, "Potato blood can make no revolution."

Among the bones that were never lonely, there is a bone of loneliness in the drifting of the city through other people's bodies. The hungry are given bones. The satisfied are given books which they held over their ears. Among the stacks, listening for novelty, guests and hosts become vulnerable to the possibility others are awake. And we inside them live like fools-in-love, unwilling to leave the room even for sustenance. Fools-in-love, wandering the stacks. And a hot tub in every library, cry the guests.

Because "taste is taste" and we are cooked. "But our compassion is hard-boiled and leaves streaks of light in the glass. Our compassion sashays in and out of unawake and forgotten. Our compassion is fuel and ash we serve to our compassion." Bolts and pulleys, ropes retrieved from other countries. Until mist and vapor emerge from the pot.

"For food like society itself suffers from an overabundance of intellect," wrote Barthes. Health is born of constraint and lassitude must be exacting, if exceedingly spare. Errors such as lyricism expand the fens we are told we shouldn't be wandering. We shouldn't be wandering among the fins and final hours. We should never wander the library where our compassion is only touring the canals and the hot tub like a hymn is only an invocation to live.

The idea that we are cooked, of course, is common, especially since dessert must always be withheld, so that we don't partake of ideas. The meal is only an effort at persuasion. But our compassion is the embarrassment of survival plus a ruthless innovation in what we are asked to metabolize—the local, by which they mean whatever is left over after patronage and between the openings—the global by which they mean a very thin layer of the ineffable. "An incandescent terror," wrote Eliot. He didn't eat bones. He chewed on pure endurance, but he didn't eat all day. Thus reaching weightlessness and translucency.

The host kisses the stains on our mouth. A moth circles the flame. A magnolia between the teeth, we are starving to repeat the scene. The menu is spelled out by fireflies and the choice is made internally through a process of which one is not aware, which coincides with no known predilections, save the instinct to carry on the assemblage.

The host says taste the sun, taste the earth. But it is all dry. Tongue to the crust of the earth. Tongue to the fringes of light. Tongue to the gesture of life. Because we lack ritual and we love emblems.

Nutrition is the canal of memory, not ours but of nutrition itself pulsing with other nutrients. "Grasping is grasping." The only true grasp is the one that reaches for all others in all directions at once. Because there are no innocent stomachs, no innocent tastes we're not sure that the only taboo is tautology. No, only habit is served and it is relentlessly broken—sliced—divided and served to itself. It is as though the meal acquires powers of autonomy, to assimilate itself against the impulse to disappear. To escape from likeness and repetition, to escape from kinship. A breath diet. A breath with no fight in it, somehow followed by an incomplete copy, never the same. Always new. Accomplishing not even a heart beat. To reach or not to reach at all or to go at it all at once like crazy—against the whole notion of the alimentary is the dailiness at the edges of the ineffable—

World within. World without. Obese worlds. Over them, around all of it. Headfirst into the paunch of silence.

Outside the hygienic gaze oozes over the scatter just as the scatter returns to the open—

Nausikaa's Isle
A Tribute to Paul Vangelisti

Even I do not exclude the operations of fortune

It does not seem right,
either at inception
or execution,
from key to hammer to string
forty-eight pieces,

well-tempered.

Like a clock.

Like something
that is not broken.

Leave ideas of gestalt.

Leave theory,
dissection,
logic,
method,

supposition.

How many things
are not broken?

I like to think the man
from the island of Cos
in the Age of Pericles
and the one from Pergamum

like you,

would have seen it too.

*

How many things
are not broken?

On the whole the winter was like springtime

And how it is
not often so
elemental slighting
of category

permitting places
out of placement,

and airs without mercury
to report.

A two-figure civilization
housed, with and
without margin

and wholly imperceptible to all.

Nausikaa's Isle
A Tribute to Paul Vangelisti

Viagra

Because even at the best of times,
the worst can happen.

Because as we grow old,
we grow more timid.

Because young women are frightening.

Because sometimes old guys who finally decide
to cash it all in on the trophy find
they don't have a hook to hang it on.

Because that old insatiable Parisian count
in Casanova—who'd spared no woman
from princess to stable girl—
was disgraceful in his dotage

when he could no longer manage
and tried, again and again, then

shrugged and wiggled his powdered ass
at the "wristband" boys, declared:
"One must make the best of any situation."

Gianluca Muratori

Lines: for a Fish out of Water

I first met Paul in 1984 at a West Los Angeles dinner party. LA seemed (to me) far from everywhere in those days, like that remote outpost in *The Desert of the Tartars*, so I was surprised to learn that Paul was not only a poet, but a translator of contemporary avant-garde Italian poetry. He was working then on the manuscript of *Villa*, and showed me a fragment of it that he had brought along to discuss with that evening's host. I was immediately taken with the poetic voice of the text, couched in the persona of the world-weary ancient Roman poet "G. Paullus Lunatus" (Paul's Italian roots are in the Lunigiana region of the Apennines).

> *I am afraid that we must look elsewhere*
> *than the self. The heart, my friend, gathers*
> *no wisdom only pain and ecstasy.*
> *One learns to treat it like a pocket,*
> *sometimes full, others almost empty,*
> *but always, one hopes, there is something*
> *for it to bear. (Villa, V)*

We started to converse. I had only recently come to California to live and work, and was still trying to get a feel for the city and the region: I knew I had a lot to learn. "Don't bother, kid," said Paul. "In my first years here I would wake up every morning, look out the window, and start to cry . . . it was so damn *depressing* to be in LA." From then on he always called me "kid," even though he was only about a decade older than me.

Paul had grown up in San Francisco's North Beach neighborhood in the years between *noir* and Beat, when the language of Italy could still be heard on the streets and in homes. He had later washed ashore in Southern California quite by chance, and was when I met him still a fish out of water there. As a professional poet-translator, Paul had to take in those days an array of part-time temporary teaching positions and odd jobs in order to make ends meet. He might cut short a phone conversation by saying cryptically, "I gotta go, kid: it's my night to teach *out on the tundra*." It was his way of referring — with a metaphor, naturally, because more than anyone I knew he loved to use figural language — to soul-crushing evening composition classes taught in community colleges at the extreme edges of LA. Nothing could keep him down for long, however, because there was always another book to translate, another poem to complete.

After a couple of years of growing friendship, Paul offered to take me deep-sea fishing with him. I hadn't known that fishing was as important to him as writing . . . but, like I said, I still had a lot to learn. Paul didn't care to go out to sea with a bunch of total strangers, so he chartered a boat for the occasion. With us came a motley crew of unemployed poets, occasionally employed Hollywood screenwriters and directors, a few French and Italian tourists passing through LA, and various academics on leave. If they were not friends of Paul's, they were friends of his friends, and that was good enough for him.

Paul picked me up as the sun began to set on a Thursday evening, and we drove to San Pedro to board the fishing boat, which would have to cross the Channel in the dead of night in order to reach Catalina Island before sunrise. She wasn't much to look at, and was named the *"Betty G."* Paul whispered to me as the passengers settled into their berths, "probably that's the name of the captain's old lady." The captain looked pretty old himself, and as though he'd just stepped off the set of *Gilligan's Island*, replete with a white beard, sunburnt face, and pot belly. It made me wonder if this craft was any more seaworthy than the *S.S. Minnow*.

Toward midnight the diesel motor coughed and roared to life, the *Betty G.* set out and, once outside the harbor breakwater, hit choppy seas and big swells in the Channel. The vessel began to pitch violently in the darkness, as gusts of wind blew noxious diesel exhaust fumes below deck. It didn't take long for the inevitable to happen. One by one, the passengers arose and staggered to the aft rail. Over the deafening roar of the motor and the wind the sound of their distress was distinctly audible. Audible, that is, to everyone except Paul, who was deeply asleep under a woolen blanket in a berth, as if he hadn't a care
in the world.

When I awoke and went up on deck toward 5 am to get ready to fish, LA had vanished from view, the motor was idling, the jet-black mass of Catalina Island loomed perhaps only a hundred yards away in the darkness, there was the nearby sound of surf, and the first glimmer of light was just appearing in the East.

Paul was already preparing his live-bait rig. He explained excitedly that the only time to catch yellowtail would be before the sun rose in the sky, at which point our fishing lines would become visible. Then, as if in a time-lapse film, the cliffs of the island began to glow red; the water suddenly turned from black to turquoise; technicolor clouds lit up in the sky; the sun was about to come up.

"Take a look at that, kid!" he shouted, pointing down at the surface of the sea. All around the boat swam schools of yellowtail, their colors shining as they flashed past us just beneath the surface, which with the coming dawn had grown glassy despite the constant motion of the ocean.

Paul occupied the best spot at the stern rail, and no one would have thought that it should have been otherwise. Wearing a battered canvas hat, he was wholly in his element. He handled his fishing line as though it were a line of verse: his fingers working it deftly, and his hands trembling ever so slightly, he caressed the nearly invisible filament with the sure touch of an artist. I only ever saw him as completely absorbed when talking with students or colleagues about writing or translating contemporary poetry. On the ocean, as at his desk, he could work magic, and the rod was —like the pen —his enchanted wand: the fish simply rose to his bait, while ignoring everyone else's. Perhaps he loved fishing so much because it was a living allegory of the poetic process, of drawing something elusive up out of the depths.

I didn't catch much of anything, either then or on later trips, but it hardly mattered. For me it was enough to be out at sea and sharing in the adventure. Indeed, much of the fun was in watching Paul cast a line as if it were the single most important thing in the world, along with writing poetry, from which it didn't really differ.

onward

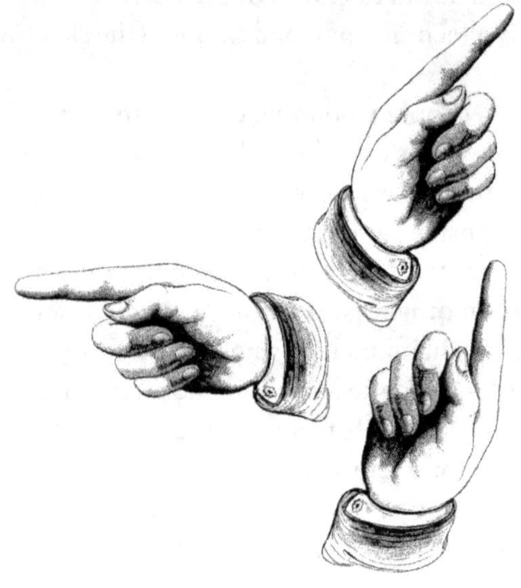

Rebecca Chamlee

Is there an Italian tradition in philosophy?

Trying to sketch a perspective on the original character of an Italian tradition in philosophy, and in order to think of it as an antidote to the increasing dominance of analytical philosophy, I'd like to emphasize some of its features, following the suggestions contained in Remo Bodei's *We Divided* (2006.)

The first feature is the approach the Italian tradition has imposed on the reading and writing of philosophical works: the philological accuracy and scruples in interpreting texts, the care for detail, the taste for a "philosophy of composition" that is able to join reason and imagination (an attitude in sharp distinction to the Anglo-Saxon tradition.)

The second feature is the civil, and not political, vocation of Italian philosophy. In an historical condition in which the State has been weak—or absent—in relation to other states, and often in the shadow of a very strong Catholic Church, Italian philosophers have played the role of political preceptors not, as Scholastic philosophers did, in favor of other philosophers or students, but in favor of non-philosophers and of the ruling classes. See, for t, Nicolò Machiavelli's work or Galileo Galilei in his Dialogue on "massimi sistemi." In development after Galilei, we have not had a deep and constant reflection on science, except for some people in Twentieth Century, like Peano, Vailati or Enriques.

The third feature is that the best of Italian philosophy comes from those areas where a restricted Cartesian logic is not predominant, where the model of exactness typical of natural sciences is not followed. And it happens in all the fields where there is a collision between two kinds of logic as, for instance, in political thought, with Nicolò Machiavelli and Antonio Gramsci; in history; with Giambattista Vico and Vincenzo Cuoco; in aesthetics with Francesco De Sanctis and Benedetto Croce. Actually, we could define Italian philosophy in toto as a "philosophy of impure reason," but also as a "civil philosophy which has not always been fearless enough to clash with political and religious authority."

We can summarize the features of Italian philosophy—also quoting Bodei—recalling that: "[it] is at its best when attempting to solve problems in which the universal and the particular, the logical and the empirical, collide. Such problems arise from the intersections of associational life and various networks, from individual conscience that combines the awareness of the limits imposed by reality with projections of desire, the opacity of historical experience with its transcriptions into images and concepts, the impotence of morality with the harshness of the world, and thought with experience. There have been thus many (successful) attempts to preserve zones of rationality in territories that appeared to have none and to make sense of forms of knowledge and practices that seemed dominated by the imponderability of arbitrariness, taste and chance."

Finally, we can notice how such a description of Italian philosophy would seem to place under the rubric of "impure reason" the affirmative task of philosophy. Yet, it must be stressed, there was not and there is not any "weakening" of the demands for intelligibility of the real; rather an effort to reclaim areas that had been too hurriedly abandoned by a form of reasoning identified with the victorious models of physical-mathematical sciences. In this sense, we can establish the idea that Italian philosophy should be considered a philosophy of "impure reason," which "takes into account the conditions, imperfections and possibilities of the world, as opposed to pure reason, which is instead concerned with a knowledge of the absolute, the immutable and the rigidly normative."

A "vaste programme" one could say, quoting Charles de Gaulle. In any case, something worth pursuing, if for no other reason than to recover the idea of poetry as a form of knowledge…

Modena, August 2014

and Augustine gazing at the invisible . . .

The photograph that follows graced the cover of *Invisible City #12* (May 1974); it is perhaps the most eloquent and unusual of the half-dozen that Robert Gumpert gave us for the magazine.

While most of those photographs centered on the miners of Harlan County (West Virginia)—in 1976, Red Hill Press published his portfolio of the same name—this photograph is a pure product of his native city.

After 40 years, the phrase from Pound's *Cantos* strikes me: "and Augustine gazing at the invisible . . ."

The gentleman in the suit is at rest on his cane, awaiting a bus. Nothing unusual in that, but the calm of the entire photo is astonishing. The towers and autos of Los Angeles form the backdrop, with an empty swath of an unknown yet familiar boulevard curving to his right. The bus has yet to arrive. The gentleman is concentrated and is, apparently, unaware of the camera. The picture seems unposed, yet superbly framed. The gentleman's entire posture is captured in the moment.

So much like the project, both poetic & political, of *Invisible City*: ". . . issued whenever enough good material is available."

Paul proposed the journal in the late summer of 1970. We were building on the *San Francisco Quarterly*, an undergraduate journal at the University of San Francisco (we'd met at that office in September 1966). "In those times," *Invisible City* would gather poetry, translations, statements and graphics. As a tabloid, it lasted from 1971 through early 1982, some 28 numbers, in 20 issues, comprising some 484 pages. In 1981, we launched a concurrent book-series, which has, so far, produced some six volumes. In 1978, we had planned an anthology of the first 25 numbers of the tabloid, for which this photo would be the cover.

Time has pushed that project aside, at least in the form contemplated. But this photo remains an emblem of what we hoped to publish: a condensation of the tabloid's energies, rendered into a compact book. "Invisible City" would float in the sky of Los Angeles.

Perhaps more than any other cover from the tabloid, this photo communicates the vision of *Invisible City*: an apparently random figure focused, albeit blind, composed amidst the cityscape of Los Angeles.

This brief note cannot be an account of the tabloid *Invisible City*. Those 484 pages portray the adventure of that journal. Suffice it to say that *Invisible City* continues, perhaps as a tabloid, perhaps as a book. Soon, we will be issuing some slight, if significant, interventions in print, using the imprint Invisible City Editions. "ICE," that is, not an agency of isolation and discipline, all too familiar in today's journalism. Rather these slight pamphlets, cards and broadsides endeavor to continue the links between readers & writers as we glide into this era, nearly 50 years after we started publishing as undergraduates in those remote but crucial years of the mid-1960s.

Cesar Vallejo wrote: "The artist should, before shouting in the streets or getting thrown in jail, create, in a tacit, silent heroism, the great, deep political aqueducts of humanity, which only the centuries make visible and fructify. . . . If the artist renounces the creation of what we should call the nebulous politics of human nature, reducing himself to the secondary and sporadic role of propaganda and the barricade itself—who will perform the great miracles of the spirit?"

Invisible City

ABOUT THE TYPE

This book is set in 12 and 14 point Arno, a typeface named for the Florentine river. Arno draws on the accessibility of early humanist types of the 15th & 16th centuries. Designed by Adobe's Robert Slimbach, Arno is in the tradition of early Venetian and Aldine book types.

Nausikaa's Isle
A Tribute to Paul Vangelisti
ed. by Dennis Phillips

Postmedia Books 2015
reprint October 2020
136 pp.
isbn 9788874901425

Postmedia Srl, Milano
www.postmediabooks.it